In Loving Memory of My Daughter,

Katherine Joann Roseberry

Forever In Our Hearts

ACKNOWLEDGMENTS

First, I want to thank God for loving me enough to entrust me to share His message with the world. Secondly, a heartfelt thank you to my children (both biological and surrogate) for loving me and keeping me on task. I Love You! Also, much love to my family for the financial support and encouragement that you have given me. Then, to the Menopause Sisters and my friends, I am grateful to God for aligning my garden with such beautiful flowers. It is a blessing to have so many people in my life who love and support me. I Love You All.

In addition, I owe so much to those individuals who shared their dreams with me. Lastly, I want to thank my publisher, Delisa Lindsey, for the work she did to help make my dream become a reality.

God moves in mysterious ways. His wonders to perform.

I made a conscience decision to not share the revelation I received from God which prompted me to write this book. I didn't want to go through life trying to convince people to believe that what I said happened actually did. I came to the conclusion, however, that whether people believed me or not that would solely be based upon their religious belief and their spiritual relationship with God. Therefore, the issue wasn't about my wants but instead it was about my obedience to God, my faith, and my trust in Him.

Since God is in control and He did instruct

me to share that particular story with you, I had to go back to include it. I believe that there is a reason why I had to write this book. God has a purpose for each individual. I am not exactly certain what His plan was when He instructed me to write this book nor do I know where I fit into that plan, but what I do know is that God makes no mistakes and that is all that matters to me. I am praying that writing this book will in some way offer me comfort and spiritual enrichment as I go through the difficult process of accepting that God has called one of His children and one of my children home.

This is how my story begins. One Sunday morning, I put a few steaks in the oven and turned the dial to 300 degrees so that they could bake slowly. I went upstairs and laid across my bed. I turned the television on and proceeded to scan the channels in search of a program that I might find interesting to watch. There was a documentary on the television station, TV1, which happens to be channel 157 on my television. Since I love watching true life stories, I began looking at it. I don't remember the title of the show nor can I recall who the documentary was about but I can tell you that the program was portraying the life of a very talented jazz musician.

The musician had become addicted to heroin. One day, he obtained these certain drugs from his supplier on credit. When he didn't pay for them, his supplier had him killed to send a message to anyone who might be thinking that they could get away with not paying. About half way through the program, a commercial came on and I decided to run downstairs to check on the steaks. I opened the oven door and peeked in. The steaks were not done yet so I ran back upstairs to continue watching the documentary hoping that I had not missed any part of the program. When I returned to my room to lay back across the bed, I noticed that the channel had been changed. The numbers *190* was in the bottom left-hand corner of the television screen.

Now, strange things have happened in my life but that was a first. I began to wonder what the heck was going on. I remember thinking, "I know that I was watching channel 157." So I immediately changed the channel back. My mind, however, was wrestling to try to come up with a logical explanation. Unable to come up with one, I decided to dismiss the incident from my thoughts and resume watching the documentary. Suddenly, I had this feeling that I needed to go back to channel 190 because I was feeling that there must have been something on that station that I was supposed to see. With that thought in mind,

I picked the remote up and punched in the numbers 1-9-0. The television was showing a still picture with a red background. The caption read, "100 Top Movies." I sat up on the side of my bed waiting for the list of the titles. I began thinking about the movies that I had seen as I began to put the titles in ranking order, wondering if I had actually been able to correctly name some of them. I waited patiently for a few minutes to see the list of names but they never appeared. The screen remained the same.

At this point, I wasn't sure what to think. Honestly, I had decided to totally erase the entire event from my memory bank. So, with that thought in mind, I went back to TV1, channel 157, to catch the ending of the program. Another commercial was on so I went back downstairs to check on the steaks. When I returned, as soon as I sat down on the side of my bed, "When I Realized That I

Would Never See You Again," popped into my head. Now, based on my past experiences, I knew that there must have been a reason that all of this was happening to me.

Since the ordeal seemed to fall into the supernatural category, I knew that I needed to ask God to reveal to me what was going on. Now that I suffer from "sometimers", I quickly grabbed my notebook and wrote the title down. For all of you who are not old enough to know what that is, "sometimers" is the stage that comes before Alzheimer's. Anyway, the blinds in my bedroom were open so I looked up toward the sky and asked, "God, what am I supposed to do with this title?" I truly can't explain but God placed in my spirit that it was to be the title of my next book.

I sat there for a moment and still peering

through the blinds I said, "Okay. So what am I supposed to write about?" It became just as clear to me that I was going the write in my daughter's voice what happens from the time that God whispers in your ear that it is time to go until you make that transformation and beyond.

I am sure that by now you are a little confused because I surely was but I am trying to relay the message to you the same way that it was relayed to me. Meanwhile, I was sitting there in a state of confusion just scratching my head. So I looked up to the sky again and I asked, "How am I supposed to do that?" Then, it was like I could hear God say, "I will never leave you nor forsake you." I suddenly knew that God had given me conformation that He wanted me to be the co-author of this book.

Within minutes I began to write. The words

were flowing through my head so quickly that I could hardly keep up. When I finally put my pencil down, I had hand-written approximately ten pages. Notwithstanding, it has taken me awhile to finish this book because I was careful to not put anything that I wasn't inspired to include in it. The results of what you are reading are specifically what I was spiritually guided to write.

I pray that my book will be a blessing to someone. Oh and by the way, I want to also share with you that there isn't even a channel 190 included in my programming package. I only discovered that fact a few days ago while re-enacting the revelation out for my friend, Madeline. As she would say, *"But God!"*

"God, grant me the serenity to accept the things that I cannot change, Courage to change the things that I can, and the Wisdom to know the difference."

The moment I realized that my earthly life, the life that I had relished for forty-two years was ending, I immediately began reflecting on the time that I had wasted. I grew up in a family that wasn't pew warmers. In other words, my family didn't go to church every time that the church doors were open but the elders in the family believed in teaching their children to respect God and to reverence Him. I was taught Bible verses and I didn't dare eat my food before blessing it nor did I go to bed before saying my prayers.

Unlike my mother, I didn't fear death. It was a wonder that I didn't develop thanatophobia, the fear of death, like my mother, because the mere thought of dying horrifies her. I think that Mommy's fear began around the age of five when her mother died. After that traumatizing experience her fear would intensify with each loss. In my life however, there had been many times when I had welcomed death.

The past several months prior to my own demise I had become so grief stricken by the loss of my daughter, Lady Alejandra (Lady Bug), that all that I wanted to do was to go where I could be with her again. My will to live had diminished. The loss of the two children who decided that they didn't want to enter this world was saddening for me. Worse though, was to lose a child whom I had actually given birth to and whom I had nurtured, cared for, and bonded with which was very devastating.

Those of you who know from firsthand experience what it is like to bury a child can relate to the depth of the pain that I was experiencing. You understand what it is like to try to deal with the emptiness that you are left with. You can truly relate to what it is to have a broken heart. I felt an inner ache that penetrated my body so deeply that I was unable to find anything that would give me relief. Therefore, like most people, I found myself desperately looking for anything that might make the pain go away, even if it was just going to last for a moment.

When I found myself in that situation, I didn't have any desire to turn to God. At that time, I saw Him as the Orchestrator of my misery so instead I turned to the bottle, a

Seagram's gin bottle to be precise. For anyone who has never had to bury their child, I pray that you will never have to come face to face with that traumatizing situation.

As I reflect, each time that the doctor told me I was going to be a mother, I would become so overjoyed. There was never the thought that perhaps one day I might have to bury one of my children. We don't expect to outlive our babies. I had personally known people who buried their children. Needless to say, you always think that these things won't happen to you. No one wants to think that it could become a reality for them. Oh, but when it did happen to me on that cold and dreary day in November, I experienced, for the first time in my life, the devastation of grief. My body immediately and totally transformed into an empty shell.

In spite of the fact that I had lost the desire

to live, to actually die would mean that I would be leaving my biological son and my three adopted daughters behind along with so many people who were near and dear to me. At that point though, I truly believed in my heart that they would eventually be okay. As I lay in my bed in what seemed to feel like a semi-conscious state, my life began to play back in my mind. It was like watching an old reel-to-reel tape. It appeared to me as if the Play button had been pushed allowing the projector to show me frame by frame re-enactments of my life. So many thoughts began to run through my mind. I was seeing autobiographical pictures of the good, the bad, and the ugly images of my lifecycle.

It was the end of July and the children were out of school on their summer break. In just two short weeks, however, they would be returning to school. It had been a tradition of mine to go shopping for school clothes and supplies the day before registration began. This year would be no exception. It was Sunday morning and I got up feeling physically weak. I had stopped drinking liquor and it had been approximately six weeks since I had turned a Seagram's gin bottle up to my lips but as my mom would say, "I was paying the piper." The alcohol had begun to make me feel physically sick.

I started drinking heavily immediately after my daughter's death. For months, I had convinced myself that drinking was what I needed to do to numb the emotional pain so that I could try to get through each day. Let me just share with you that putting a Band-Aid over a sore is never a viable solution. It will only serve as a temporary fix. To mask your problems might provide a treatment, but not a cure.

My children began coming into my room one by one to coax me to get up. They were anxious to go school shopping and then to dinner. Since I knew that I wasn't going to be able to get out of the promise that I had made to them, I phoned my mom and persuaded her to accompany me on my quest. Upon arrival to the mall, an indescribable driving force consumed my body and I found myself propelling in and out of stores trying to purchase four outfits of clothing and a pair of tennis shoes for each of my children for the start of a new school year.

Since it was Sunday the stores opened late, around noon and closed early, around six o'clock. We were standing outside the mall doors when the attendant turned the key to unlock them. I was still scrambling to find one more outfit when the sales representative made an announcement, "The store will be closing in fifteen minutes. Please make your final selections and head up front to the cashiers." Now for the average shopper, that announcement would have been enough to have them dashing to the front of the store to pay for their merchandise and be on their way. But to an obsessive, compulsive, bipolar combined with assertiveness kind of woman such as myself, the announcement simply meant that there would be at least two more to follow before the store threatened you by turning off most of the lights. "Well, they can turn off the lights", I thought. "I simply am not leaving this store until I find one more pair of pants for my eldest daughter, who was being difficult."

The other children made their selections and loved the fact that they had not been limited to the sale rack. We finally exited the store twenty minutes after closing and one pair of pants short. Normally, after a shopping trip, we would decide on a fun place to eat. Generally, it would be a place like Greatimes or Dave & Buster's. Those were two of the most popular eateries where my children loved to play games, ride bumper cars, win prizes, and eat lots of pizza but for the first time, I was going to break tradition.

The several hours of indecisiveness and grumbling had worn me to a frazzle. Pain had begun to radiate throughout my body and I was starting to feel extremely tired. Mommie kept asking me what was wrong because my face was now showing signs of exhaustion. Every muscle and joint in my body was aching. Needless to say, I made the decision to have my mother take me where I could get something that we could take home and eat. After much deliberation, we made a family decision to order pizza and hot wings from Pizza Hut. Mommie dropped us off at home and went on her way.

Immediately after I ate dinner, I went directly upstairs to take my medicine and retire to bed. Since my bedroom was directly across the hall from the girls' bedroom I could easily hear them arguing. I determined that I was not about to play referee this time because I had another long day ahead of me which I certainly was not looking forward to. I knew that I would be getting up early the next morning to make sure that we were all dressed and ready to leave the house by eight o'clock.

The schools' registration began at nine o'clock sharp and I had four schools to go to before the task would be complete. The lines were generally long and the process could be quite lengthy. Based on my past experiences, I knew that it would more than likely take between five to six hours to get through the mounds of paperwork.

This is the day which the LORD hath made; we will rejoice and be glad in it. Psalm 118:24

The following morning, I woke up early enough to see the sunrise. I remember thinking that it had been a long time since I had actually witnessed the beauty of the sun rising above the horizon. The sky appeared to be a brighter red color than I had ever seen before. The house was quiet; everyone was still asleep. I decided that it would be a wonderful opportunity to just lie in my bed and enjoy the tranquility before the troops were called to order. I just relaxed and planned the day out in my mind.

Still feeling a little under the weather, I was

so happy that Mommie had said that she would accompany us. Since I had four schools to go to, I mapped out a route that would provide us with the least amount of back tracking. Normally, I would have cooked breakfast for my children, but not this morning. I was going to surprise everyone and take them to McDonald's for breakfast.

Mommie arrived thirty minutes later than the time we had agreed upon. She simply was not anxious to spend another long day with my bickering children. We had gone downstairs and were standing near the door when she pulled up. Once we loaded up, all that I kept praying was that I would have a better day than I had the day before. We went to breakfast and the children ordered their usual items but I couldn't seem to find anything on the menu that appealed to my taste buds. I just wasn't hungry. My only desire was to get to the first school so that I could get started on my task.

After everyone finished eating, we headed out to my eldest daughter's school. Then, one by one, I was able to complete the registration process for each one of my children. I was feeling relieved to know that everything had been done so that they could start their first day back to school with no problems. I was thankful that God had given me the strength to complete the task. However, the standing and waiting in those long lines had taken a tremendous toll on my body. Each time that I got back into the van, Mommie would look at me and ask, "Are you okay?" Too tired to speak, I would just nod my head and lay back in the seat but my mother knew me better than anyone else.

Mommie and I were best friends. I shared things with her that I wouldn't share with anyone else, except God, of course. We saw each other every day and we talked on the phone several times a day. I was never able to hide behind the mask that I so often wore for the rest of the world to hide my inner feelings. For those very reasons, she knew that something was wrong.

It was about six o'clock when the children and I finally arrived back home. Barely unable to climb down out of the van, I slowly walked to the door, unlocked it, and went up the stairs to bed. I took my pain medicine and I saw my journal at the foot of my bed. While I lay there waiting for my medicine to kick in, I penned a journal entry. Of course, had I known that it was going to be my final entry I would have written so much more. Afterwards I said my prayers. Even though physically it had been a challenging day, I was thankful that I was able to achieve my goals. Before I knew it, I had fallen asleep.

When Mommie made her routine call to inform me that she had made it home safely, I didn't even hear the phone ring.

While I was in slumber land, I had a dream. In my dream, I was in a place that I wasn't quite familiar with. I was clothed in all white and I found myself just wandering around searching for anything or anybody that I might recognize so that I would feel safe but there was no one there besides me. The area was so desolate. When I awoke from the dream, I reached over and grabbed my phone. I saw that I had missed Mommie's call. When I called her back it was around nine o'clock. I was still in excruciating pain so I kept our conversation short. As I reflect, it is so hard to imagine now how my mother and I could spend the entire day together and still find so much to talk about later on the telephone. That night, though, I didn't have any desire to talk to her or anyone else for that matter.

As much as I tried to conceal my agony from my mother, she could still tell that something was wrong. I told her that I was in excruciating pain. My thought was, "If I could somehow manage to just get to sleep that perhaps the morning might offer me a new perspective." Mommie admonished me to get some rest and she assured me that she would be over bright and early to check on me. My mother always ended her telephone conversations with, "I love you", but for the first time, I said it to her before she could say it to me. We said our good-byes and I hung the phone up.

I know now that God was giving me what Mommie refers to as "peek time." She believed that when people were dying that God granted them the opportunity to say their good-byes or to mend any broken fences they might have. I believe that there could definitely be something to that concept. If you truly give it some thought, I am certain that you might recall seeing or hearing about someone who was terminally ill and hanging on by a very thin thread appear to suddenly get better and then they died. Maybe it was just as Mommie had said. At any rate, I am thankful that my "peek time" was shared with my mother. The very thought that the last memory she will be left with is my expression of endearment makes me so happy. It was God's way of showing her love.

I sincerely hope that when my mother has had time to reflect that she realizes that God gave us both the desires of our hearts. I needed to let my mother know that even though we have waded through troubled waters, I loved her so very much and I knew that she loved me. The saying, "give people their flowers while they are living" should be a daily practice. Kind words and deeds should be what you want to extend to those people in your life that you profess to love. "I just called to say that I love you," could mean so much to a person, especially, if they are experiencing some type of crisis in their life. 1 Corinthians 13:13 tells you how important love is. *"And now these three remain: faith, hope and love. But the greatest of these is love."*

If you haven't been in the habit of taking the time to show those people in your life that you care, start now. Where there is breath, there is life and where there is life, there is opportunity. Don't be left with should've, would've, or could've baggage strapped to your back because you waited too late to reach out to those who you love. Remember the word of God says in Galatians 5:14, *"For all the law is fulfilled in one word, even in this; Thou shalt love thy neighbour as thyself."* My great-great grandmother used to say, "Charity begins at home." The truth of the matter is if you are having trouble starting there, at home, I hardly see how you would be able to extend love to others.

I could feel myself dozing off. I hadn't quite gotten to the REM stage of sleep when this weird feeling came over me. As I began to feel my vital organs shutting down and while breath was leaving my body, the Serenity Prayer popped into my thoughts. I began to recite it over and over in my mind.

God grant me the serenity to accept the things I cannot change; courage to change the things I can; and wisdom to know the difference. Living one day at a time; enjoying one moment at a time; accepting hardships as the pathway to peace; taking, as He did, this sinful world as it is, not as I would have it; trusting that He will make all things right if

I surrender to His Will; that I may be reasonably happy in this life and supremely happy with Him forever in the next. Amen.

Our mother frequently recited the Serenity Prayer to us. It was a prayer that she lived by with the exception of the idea of death. I never could understand how Mommie could exhibit so much faith in her day to day life and yet not believe that there had to be something better beyond this earthly life. I was convinced at a young age that there was a better life that awaited me. My belief was that the trials and tribulations that we endure on earth were simply tests. I also believed that if you could pass those tests then there would be a reward that would be waiting for you. It was inconceivable to think that you would struggle to live a Godly life and that there would not be some kind of payoff.

Watch therefore, for you do not know what hour your Lord is coming. But know this, that if the master of the house had known what hour the thief would come, he would have watched and not allowed his house to be broken into. Therefore you also be ready, for the Son of Man is coming at an hour you do not expect.

Matthew 24:42-44

My body began to feel weightless. If you can envision a feather as the wind gently glides it slowly back and forth in mid-air, then you will have some idea of what my body was feeling at that moment. Suddenly, there was this radiant light. I knew that I was seeing the light with my mind's eye because it absolutely wasn't humanly possible to peer into a light that shined so brightly with the naked eye. I wondered if the fact that everything was so bright was a good sign. Could it perhaps mean that I had actually done some things in life that had pleased God? "Are the people that displease God surrounded by darkness when they die?" I asked myself.

It didn't appear that I was in any particular place. I did not see no rooms, no doors, no people, nor could I hear any sound. "Is this another dream?" I thought. Then suddenly it became apparent to me that the hour glass had been turned over and the sand was slowly trickling down. The only thing that I saw was a tunnel that seemed to endlessly go on and on for as far as I could see. At this point, I still wasn't exactly certain what was happening to me. My mind was scrambling to try to make some kind of sense out of the ordeal. It felt to me as if I had stepped outside of my body and that I was standing on the side of my bed just looking down at myself but, at that very moment, God softly whispered in my ear that it was time for me to go.

One thought that I had, well actually to be quite honest it was more of a concern, was that my mother would never be able to get over my death. You would have to understand my mother's makeup. Mommie is such an emotional creature. She cries about everything. Talk about wearing your emotions on your sleeve? She wears her emotions on both arms. I was so happy that I didn't inherit that characteristic from her but my youngest brother, Tony, was just like Mommie. I was convinced that he too would have a very difficult time moving on with his life after my death. Now, my son and my eldest brother, Millard, would mourn but I felt that they would be able to go on.

Millard seemed to have a better acceptance and understanding than any of the rest of my immediate family about death. We always found that astonishing since he was the one who was mentally challenged. Of course that goes to show you that God will compensate for any losses that we have. I have seen people who could read the Bible yet they lacked the ability to recognize their own name on paper.

Nevertheless, life goes on and my family would have to learn how to go on living their lives without me. Since my mother is the person who everyone will look to for strength, I hope and pray that she will look to God to help her get through this difficult time. I don't want my loved ones to spend their lives grieving for me. I know that they will experience some sadness due to my death but I am truly okay. People say that time heals all wounds. That is an inevitable fact. You may be left with a permanent emotional scar but the wound will eventually get better as time goes on and in due time the pain will subside.

On earth, I struggled daily to acquire some kind of peace in my life. I constantly found myself dealing with emotional and spiritual turmoil. I realize now that had I put my trust in God that my burdens would have been much lighter. Once people realize that they don't have to always be in control, they will learn to actually take their burdens to the Lord and leave them there. Here I have finally found the peace that I had searched for most of my earthly life. I now have eternal peace. Psalm 55:22 says, *"Cast thy burden upon the LORD, and He shall sustain thee: He shall never suffer the righteous to be moved."*

It had never been my plan to just quietly slip away. I never wanted to die alone. But God is in control. He determines the day that we come into the world that I left behind and He determines the day that we enter into this world. So that is exactly how I left earth, quickly and quietly. I am very grateful though that God loved me enough to not allow me to suffer a painful nor agonizing death. I thank Him for being merciful enough to spare me and my family from having to hopelessly and helplessly stand by and watch me suffer.

I have seen a few people die in my lifetime and I have witnessed some of them linger for hours and even days. I used to wonder if they held on because they were waiting for something or someone. Maybe they just couldn't bear to leave their earthly body. Of course, there was always that remote possibility that they were in no hurry to be introduced to the fire and brimstone. Now that's a scary thought, fire and brimstone.

It is absolutely impossible for me to tell you why other people held on but I can certainly tell you why I wasn't quite ready to surrender. I had so many questions that I was still trying to answer. Questions like: Had I kept God's Ten Commandments? Well, to answer that question honestly, I would have to say that most of the time I tried to obey God's laws. Did I treat people the way that I wanted to be treated? Well, to tell you the truth, not always. I seldom found myself using the, "turn the other cheek," approach. I usually practiced the "law of retaliation, an eye for an eye." Did I love God with all of my heart? Absolutely! Now there was certainly no question about that.

That brings me to another thought written in John 14:15 where Jesus tells Philip, *"If you love Me, keep My commandments."* Why hadn't I done that? After searching my heart, I couldn't seem to come up with an answer. I had plenty of excuses though. So many people try to bend the word of God to justify their behavior. My favorite saying in this scenario was, "the spirit is willing but the flesh is weak." I am sure that some of you are quite familiar with that old cliché. I certainly said it too, many times, to justify my actions.

Now the question was: Why didn't I instead practice my great-grand mother's teachings? She would tell me whenever I went to her with a moral dilemma, "What would Jesus say? What would Jesus do?" Grandma coined those phrases long before they became a slogan printed on baseball caps and tee shirts. Proverbs 1:5 tells us, *"A wise man will hear and increase in learning, And a man of understanding will acquire wise counsel."* I can only conclude from that verse that a foolish man will not learn from their mistakes but instead will press the gas paddle of their car to the floor and spin their tires in the mud very fast only to end up in the same spot. Some of you know exactly what I am talking about.

I had been told by my elders my entire life that Jesus commands us to love the Lord and each other. I had read the written instructions in Matthew 22:37-38, *"Jesus said to him, "You shall love the Lord your God with all your heart, with all your soul, and with all your mind. This is the first and great commandment."* That was the only thing I thought that I just might have come close to getting right. But to love the Lord is to be obedient to Him. My strong will and arrogance frequently made it difficult to be totally submissive, even to God.

The fact that I had said that I loved God with my mouth and in my heart believed that I loved Him though I didn't always show my love with my actions left me feeling ashamed. I knew right from wrong. I had attended church and Sunday school. I frequently studied my Bible therefore; I really didn't have an excuse for my ungodly behavior. Although I was quite aware of what the Bible said, I had not always applied those teachings to my daily walk with Christ. My advice to you is to strive to not merely talk the talk, but for you to diligently strive to walk the walk. Matthew 5:16 says, "Let your light shine before men in such a way that they may see your good works, and glorify your Father who is in heaven."

But in accordance with your hardness and with your impenitent heart you are treasuring up for yourself wreath in the day of wreath and revelation of the righteous judgment of God, who "will render to each one according to his deeds" eternal life to those who by patient continuance in doing good seek for glory, honor, and immortality; but to those who are self-seeking and do not obey the truth, but obey unrighteousness-indignation and wrath, tribulation and anguish, on every soul of man who does evil, of the Jew first and also of the Greek; but glory, honor, and peace to everyone who works what is good, to the Jew first and also to the Greek. For there is no partiality with God. Romans 2:5-11

Many thoughts were flooding my head. One thought that I had was that I was still wearing a brightly lit neon sign that read, "Still Under Construction." I began evaluating my life and sort of weighing the pros and cons. For the first time in my life, I was worried about dying. What seemed to concern me the most was my spiritual relationship with God. I had done a lot of good deeds but now I was wondering if the good that I had done was enough to outweigh the bad. I wondered how God would measure my deeds. Had I done enough that He would find favor in me? What was so troubling for me was the fact that I couldn't honestly say "yes" to that question.

According to the Bible, God is a forgiving and a merciful God but my record was blemished. I wondered if I had done enough to wipe the slate clean or was it still too streaked from the chalky residue that I had not cleaned up? I wanted to surrender yet I was still soul searching. Had I done anything that God had not forgiven me for? I questioned that even though at this point it wasn't going to really matter because it was too late to worry about any of that now. There was no way to go back and try to get it right.

I was suddenly reminded of a quote that my philosophical brother, Tony, had posted one day on his Facebook page. He said, "Life is not like a video game. It does not offer you another life or an opportunity to start over." I couldn't have said it any better. Your time on earth is precious. Most people waste it. I wasted it but you should use it wisely because time can be a "friendly foe," which is another one of Tony's quotes. The English writer, Edward Young, coined the phrase, "Procrastination is the thief of time." That is so true. It will rob you of the time that should be spent with God. It could rob you of time that could be spent with your loved ones. It can surely even rob you of your salvation.

Don't do what I did. I thought that I still had time to put my life back on the right track. People arrogantly live their lives like they are in control. They plan for tomorrow, next week, and even next year. The truth of the matter is that you might not even need to make plans for the next minute or even the next second. Since you are unable to predict when the battery will stop in your biological clock, my advice to you is to live each moment as if it were your last.

One thing that I want to convey to the loved ones that I left behind is that it is imperative that you get your lives together while you are still on that side and have time. Stop thinking that you can put off for tomorrow what you need to do today. It is no harder to do the right thing than it is to do the wrong thing. I can remember hearing people say that it was easier to do wrong but once again those are the people who want to justify their behavior. We learn to mix black and white to create grey areas in our lives but you cannot straddle the fence. With God, it is either good or bad, right or wrong, ugly or cute and everybody knows that God doesn't like ugly. Like so many of you, my lack of total surrender to God's will made me a straddler.

I had to be honest with myself and admit that I had not done my best to serve God nor to keep His commandments. However, even if I wasn't going to make it through those pearly gates and I went to hell instead, I hoped that God would know that I realize now that I didn't take the precious life He gave me seriously. If that was going to be the case, of course I was praying hard that it wouldn't be, I didn't think that I had lived my life so poorly that I was going to burn in hell. Of course, I didn't expect to hear the words, "Well done you good and faithful servant." I thought the very worst case scenario might be that I could find myself posted at the door, a greeter perhaps. You know, sort of like the person who directs the lost souls to the fiery furnace.

"To everything there is a season, and a time to every purpose under the heaven: A time to be born and a time to die; a time to plant, and a time to pluck up that which is planted; A time to kill, and a time to heal; a time to break down, and a time to build up; A time to weep, and a time to laugh; a time to mourn and a time to dance." Ecclesiastes 1:1-4

Death is a process. If you have ever been around an individual with a terminal illness and was dying, you might have been able to see some of the stages that the body might go through to prepare you for your journey. For example, the person generally begins to eat less and to sleep more. They frequently can be seen communicating with a loved one that has already passed on. This is God's way of preparing that individual to gradually become unaccustomed to their earthly life. It is also His way to give those loved ones who will be left behind a way to prepare themselves for the inevitable. Of course, death is not something that people seem to be able to prepare themselves for nor are individuals rarely able to immediately accept the loss of a loved one. The anticipation of a loss makes no more difference in how a person reacts than when an individual dies suddenly, as it was in my case.

I can personally testify to you that it is certainly a fact that each individual has an appointed time and you will live until that calendar date. Death knocked on my door three times in my lifetime. Those false alarms introduced me little by little to the idea that we all are just passing through this world. With each experience, I was given a tiny glimpse into what awaited me beyond this life but this time would be different. I had struck out and now I was about to embark upon my final destination. With that being said the only thing that was left for me to do was to recite the Lord's Prayer. *"After this manner therefore pray ye: Our Father which art in heaven, Hallowed be thy name. Thy kingdom come. Thy will be done in earth, as it is in heaven. Give us this day our daily bread. And forgive us our debts, as we forgive our debtors. And lead us not into temptation, but deliver us from evil: For thine is the kingdom, and the power, and the glory, for ever. Amen."* Matthew 6:9-13.

"And as it is appointed for men to die once, but after this the judgment." Hebrews 9:27.

While I was lying on the living room floor, the paramedics worked diligently to no avail for hours to perform CPR on my lifeless body. It was really pointless because I was beyond the point of no return. My spirit had already departed the earthly shell that it had been housed in for over forty years. I could hear and see my children crying as they tried to cling to hope. I had not taught them to pray no more than the ritualistic prayers that most parents teach their children. You know the bedtime prayers that most children recite with no feeling and the prayers that you are taught as a child to say when you bless your food. They were the same prayers that I had been taught as a child to say.

If prayer was what I needed to be sent up to heaven to be redeemed, I certainly did not stand a chance of being revived. Mommie's faith wasn't going to bail me out either. I mention this to impress upon you three very important facts. The first fact is that prayer is essential to God. The reason that it is important is because it is the way that we commune with God. When you pray, you are recognizing the fact that God is in control. You are acknowledging to God that you realize where your help comes from and that you know He is in charge.

The second fact is it is important that parents teach their children how to pray. In the book of Matthew chapter 6, you will find specific instructions on how to pray. Verses 5-7 in particular tell you, *"When you pray, you are not to be like the hypocrites; for they love to stand and pray in the synagogues and on the street corners so that they may be seen by men. Truly I say to you, they have their reward in full. But you, when you pray, go into your inner room, close your door and pray to your Father who is in secret, and your Father who is in secret, and your Father who sees what is done in secret will reward you.*

But when ye pray, use not vain repetitions, as the heathen do: for they think that they shall be heard for their much speaking."

Finally, it is important that you learn to accept God's will when you pray and ask Him for something. Romans 13:1 says, *"Let everyone be subject to the governing authorities, for there is no authority except that which God has established. The authorities that exist have been established by God."* When you accept God's will, you are exhibiting faith and trusting God in all matters.

Let me reiterate in hopes of making one thing perfectly clear to everyone. It is absolutely imperative to understand that we must learn to accept God's will whatever it is. We must understand that when we think that our prayer wasn't answered, no answer might just have been the answer. For instance, if an individual prays for a terminally ill relative's recovery and the person dies, we feel that God didn't answer our prayers. We usually are angry with God especially if we believe that we have been faithful servants and deserve to have our prayers answered but suppose the person whom you were praying for was praying to go be with God. That is why people need to pray to accept the will of God and acknowledge that God always knows best. People need to learn to **"Let Go and Let God!"**

Matthew 7:7 reads, *"Ask, and it will be given to you; seek, and you will find; knock and it will be open to you."* As a young adult, I believed that whatever I asked God for that I could expect to get it. When I became older and wiser, I learned that people should be careful and give great thought to what they ask God for. I came to realize that what we want isn't always what we need. I eventually came to understand that God knew better than I did what my needs were. Finally, when I read the verses before and after that particular verse, I understood that Jesus was teaching the multitudes of people who had come to see Him moral lessons. They were lessons that were expected to be handed down from generation to generation. They were examples of pure love and not a lesson in begging.

Another point comes to mind. Some people read the Bible and try to bend the word to suit them. They also tend to extract only what fits into their justifiable means. You can attempt to make God's word fit into your framework but Matthew 24:35 tell us that, *"Heaven and earth shall pass away, but my words shall not pass away."* Mommie would tell me, "If it is not broke, don't try to fix it." God doesn't need a carpenter. He is one.

There is nothing in your life that He can't fix if you will only let Him. If you are uncertain as to the meaning of anything that you read in the Bible, pray and ask God for understanding. Take heed to what the word tells us in Proverbs 3:5. *"Trust in the LORD with all thine heart; and lean not unto thine own understanding."* I would like to just add, lean not unto anyone else's understanding either. Sometimes we find ourselves buying into man's doctrine because we become mesmerized by their gift for gab and their charismatic demeanor but don't be deceived.

Delight yourself also in the LORD, And He shall give you the desires of your heart.

Psalms 37:4

Once I had totally transformed and my spirit had completely separated from my earthly body, I had never in my life felt such peace. The best description I can give you of what it is like here would be to say that it is like another earth except there is no sickness, suffering, and no death. People are happy here. I was happy. Before I arrived at my destination, I was greeted by those loved ones who died before me. When I saw them I knew that God's love is unwavering.

God knows the desires of our hearts. I was never more convinced of that then when I saw my baby, Lady Bug. On the other hand, I was worried about the fact that Jesus was not there to greet me. I wondered if it meant that He was angry with me. Perhaps I had done some things that hadn't pleased Him and that I hadn't asked for forgiveness. Needless to say, I advise you to immediately make your wrongs, right.

Can you imagine my excitement when I saw my daughter walking toward me? I had never seen her walk. The word of God came to mind from 2 Corinthians 5:16-17. It reads, *"Therefore from now on we recognize no one according to the flesh; even though we have known Christ according to the flesh, yet now we know Him in this way no longer. Therefore if anyone is in Christ, he is a new creature; the old things passed away; behold, new things have come."*

When I Realized That I Would Never See You Again

When Lady Bug was just two months old, I had to rush her to the emergency room. In the process of the staff trying to figure out what was wrong with her they caused her to develop an infection. The infection didn't allow her blood to clot, therefore her brain, lungs, and anything that would bleed did. As a result, she had three strokes. The strokes left her unable to walk or talk. To see my daughter's miraculous transformation gave me so much joy which was when I was certain that I had done some good deeds during my life on earth that was pleasing to God.

When Lady Bug came to greet me, she didn't come alone. My other two children were with her. I had lost two children prior to giving birth to Lady Bug. In life, I never even knew what sex they were. I had no idea what they looked like. But the spirit is a powerful energy and I knew them and they knew me. Here we were, all together again. Those things that we lose and those loved ones whom we feel are taken away from us on earth are eternally with us forever in the next world.

In my earthly flesh, I questioned God's love many times. Those feelings were not more evident than when I lost my children. At one time in my life, I had known that God loved me because He showed me so many times that He loved me. I could feel God's love when I would feel lonely. I could see His love every time that I saw a way being made out of no way but after my daughter died I couldn't feel anything. I couldn't feel my mother's love nor did I feel the love of my children or family and I definitely wasn't feeling any love from God. Nevertheless, sometimes God was there, banging at my door but my pain won't allow Him to come in.

Mommie always says that everything happens for a reason. It made no sense to me then how she could think that I would be able to accept that explanation at a time when I was feeling the most emotional pain that I had ever felt in my life. It seemed a bit insensitive to me at that particular time to tell me to accept the loss of my child as fate but once I got over being angry with God, I began to pray to Him for strength, peace, and understanding. Of course, what I was eventually able to accept was that what my mother said was so true. God does know best.

I realize now that God took my daughter first because He knew my time on earth was winding down. Had God taken me first, my mother would have had the responsibility of caring for Lady Bug and God promises that He will put no more on you than you can bear. To show you that God is a loving God with the patience of Job, He softened my heart and when I died, we were on good terms again. I am pleased to say that those children who preceded me in death have a place in Heaven and I need only worry about the child that I have left behind.

Usually we want to be in charge. We think that we can handle things ourselves but when we do take matters into our own hands and things don't come out the way we planned them, then we seek a scapegoat. We have to find someone to shift the blame on and you don't care who it is that you put on the hook as long as it takes you off the hook. People don't hesitate to blame God for their misfortunes either rather than to assume responsibility for their dilemmas. We don't want to take ownership for our poor choices.

How many times have you said, "It must have been God's will?" Do you think that it is His will that we be disobedient or that we choose not to follow His teachings? Of course it is not. Some of us won't take our burdens to the Lord and leave them there because we fear that He may not resolve the matter to suit us. We fear that His answer won't be what we are hoping for. We truly believe that we are the captains of our vessels. How foolish to think that when you can't even control your heart beat or your brain?

While I am on the subject of fear, I want Mommie and others like her who possesses the demon of fear to understand that it is a trick of Satan to keep them in bondage. Where I am there is absolutely nothing to fear. Of course, I can't tell you what awaits you if you end up in the dark place; therefore my advice to the living is to work on getting closer to God. As you develop a spiritual relationship with God, your spirit will be convicted to do what is pleasing to Him. If it does not, my advice to you would be to examine yourself.

"Come to Me, all you who labor and are heavy laden, and I will give you rest. Take My yoke upon you and learn from Me, for I am gentle and lowly in heart, and you will find rest for your souls. For My yoke is easy and My burden is light." Matthew 11:28-30

Man has created stumbling blocks in their life by making it seem so difficult to serve God. Religion might be complex but spirituality is not. There are some people who confuse the two and there are others who think that they are one and the same but they are not the same. Religion incorporates many man-made rules. Spirituality does not. God only has one rule and that is *"The Golden Rule."* Of course He does have specific requirements for man to meet but you can obey the Ten Commandments, believe in the Beatitudes, and follow the Golden Rule, but none of that will matter unless you heed the instructions in Romans 10:9, *"That if you confess with your mouth the Lord Jesus and believe in your heart that God has raised Him from the dead, you will be saved."*

There are so many lessons to be learned here. In this world, you learn to develop your spirituality. God teaches you to develop the ability to practice agape love which is the greatest gift that one could ever possess. The lessons taught here reach far beyond those that are taught on earth. Here in this world, your only desires are to get closer to God and to communicate with the loved ones you left behind. You see, we miss you just as much as you miss us.

We are always trying to let you know that we are with you. Our efforts to communicate with you are frequently explained as coincidences. The best scenario that I can give to help you understand would be the radio. When you turn your radio on it picks up the air waves. Those signals are not visible to the naked eye yet they are there. Well, spiritual communication works in the same manner. Of course, you have to turn your spiritual dial on to receive God's messages. Your receptors can only be strengthened through prayer and meditation.

We can only communicate with you if it is God's will that we do so and if it is your desire to communicate with us. On earth, you are allowed to have freewill but here it is

God's way or the highway. Satan can certainly vouch for that. The only desire that we long to have here is to please God. Those who seek other pleasures don't reside here. I have no idea where they are and I don't want to know either.

"And in the last days it shall be, God declares, that I will pour out my Spirit on all flesh, and your sons and your daughters shall prophesy, and your young men shall see visions, and your old men shall dream dreams." Acts 2:17

Since I had reconnected with my loved ones who had preceded me in death, it was now time to reconnect with my earthly family. There were many things that I wanted to convey to them. More importantly, there were so many things that they needed to know. I wanted to help my mother overcome her fear of death, if that was even possible. My spirit yearned to dwell where she was. I desired to be around everyone whom I had left behind.

The one way that I knew to communicate with my family and friends was through dreams. It would be a way to give them messages. I was hoping that I would be able to give them advice, small glimpses into my new world, and possibly even offer them comfort through their dreams. Most importantly, I would be able to let them know that I am always with them. So, for those reasons, my visits were calculated. It was for that very reason that I didn't go to visit my mother first. However, I made my presence known in other ways. God orchestrated my visits so that the messages would be helpful to her in her efforts to write this book.

For those of you who do not believe that we are able to communicate with our loved ones through their dreams, I would suggest that you read Luke 1:37. You will find that it says, *"For nothing will be impossible with God."* If you believe in His word, then ask yourself why you don't believe that God is omnipotent. He can do what He wishes, when He decides, where He chooses, to whom He wants, how He sees fit. I am not talking to those of you who think that you rule this universe. Nor am I speaking to those of you who think that their money and power makes them a god. Your money might buy you a seat on that shuttle that is going to Mars but that is as close to Heaven as you will get.

Mommie is quite aware of my existence. I have visited her every birthday and every holiday. I particularly come and comfort her when I feel her sadness and when she is sick. With each person whom I have visited, I have sent Mommie messages. I am sure that you are asking yourself why I didn't just go directly to her with the messages. The simplest way that I can explain it is to reiterate to you that God is in control. When He wants you to know something, He tells you in His time. He tells you exactly what He wants you to know and He delivers the message however He chooses. I don't question God and neither should you.

There are times when God comes directly to you. Then there are times when He uses others to relay His messages. The message can be delivered through a Sunday sermon or it can even come from out of the mouth of a babe. However, the message is delivered is irrelevant but what I am trying to get you to understand is that it is delivered on a "need to know" time frame.

I was adamant about giving the people whom I came back to see important information to pass on to my mother. I was cautious to communicate the same information with slight deviations. The reason for that was to insure that their message would be believable. The plan was orchestrated by God. The intricate pieces would all come together at a later date.

The first person whom I visited was a guy who I met in an online chat room during one of my sleepless nights. His name is John but I referred to him as my internet husband. I gave him that nickname because we were always having these long intellectual debates and disagreements. Most of our discussions stemmed around religious beliefs and practices. He is a very spiritual man and I learned a lot from him although I never admitted that to him. I knew that Mommie wouldn't probably think to get in touch with him after my death. She knew that I talked to him but she never met him and I didn't speak of him often like I did the people that she knew who were in my circle of friends.

I came to him with such energy and I didn't come alone. I was accompanied by an angel. The main purpose I had for visiting him was to make him aware of my death. Secondly, I wanted to send my mother a message through him. When I visited him in his dream, I began by informing him of my passing and relaying to him the details of my death. I told him that I had died of an accidental drug overdose. I explained to him that I went to sleep and that I simply didn't wake up. I knew that whenever God connected John with my mother and he shared his dream with her she would know that it was genuine because he would not have any way of knowing about the details of my death. My mother didn't even know what the cause of death was until she received the coroner's report some months later.

I went on to describe to him what life was like in my new world and what God had in store for him. God had shown me that John was going to do great things. I told him to tell my family that I was sorry that I had to go but it was my time to go. I impressed upon him that it was important to tell them how sorry I was for leaving them but that I would always be watching over them. I also shared with him my good news. I told him that I had been reunited with my daughter and how extremely overjoyed that reunion had made me. I didn't mention my other children because we had never talked about the fact that I loss two other children.

Most importantly, I shared with John that I was learning a lot from God. I explained to him that in the world that I am in now, you are given an opportunity to work on those things that you didn't quite get right while on earth, in particular your spiritual relationship with God. I wanted to make sure he understood that I was not in heaven. I am not certain that I will make it to heaven although to make it into heaven and actually sit next to God is my hope and prayer. I am working hard to get there but for now I am at peace with knowing that if God wasn't going to give me a second chance, I wouldn't be here.

The easiest way to explain this to you would be to compare the architecture of this place to a skyscraper. You know that it consists of many floors. Well, heaven would be considered the penthouse. Only God can decide on what level your soul should be. I cannot go up to join those souls that I am connected with through our earthly journey. However, they are permitted to come here to visit and be with me. One of the things that I am learning is how to totally surrender to the "will of God." Here, the soul no longer has to wrestle with the desires of the flesh. Nor does the soul have to battle with the mind for the soul has always known where it belonged and to whom it belonged. Don't misunderstand, we still have freewill. The difference is that there are fewer distractions here. There are no cell phones, televisions, computers, or any other devices that we allowed ourselves to be consumed with when we were on earth.

It was the fact that God allowed man to have "freewill" that created the battle between the spirit and the flesh. That is why going to church is an option but having church in you is a choice. In other words, going to church regularly doesn't necessarily make you closer to God. I explained to John that it is imperative that people develop their spiritual relationship with God while they are on earth. It's easier.

It was time for me to go back but I wasn't done. I had so much more to tell him but it would have to wait. It was awhile before I visited anyone else but the next person whom I visited was Charlene. I called her (Cher). We met in the mid nineties when I worked for the telephone company and we became friends. Cher and I didn't talk frequently nor did we visit each other often but we had a very unique relationship. Although we seldom could come to an agreement on most topics that we discussed, we learned to agree to disagree.

Cher has a heart of gold and that was what I loved about her. She was compassionate beyond belief and generous to a fault. There were limitations attached to my generosity. If I permitted you to enter into the circle that I had created then there was nothing that I wouldn't do for you. Of course, since I didn't have much tolerance for mankind, the circumference of my circle remained small. I was like my mother in that sense. She would say, "Everyone can't be my friend."

In spite of the love that Cher and I had for each other, there were many times when our love was over shadowed by our actions. We allowed Satan to create division using our head-strong and stubborn natures. We were both Capricorns. Sometimes our stubbornness would keep us apart for months and even years but when we would finally swallow our pride and put our differences aside, we would talk like it had been just yesterday since we had spoken to each other.

Mommie always stayed in touch with Cher. She would scold me when I was not willing to be the first one to pick up the phone and make amends. I use to think that Mommie loved everybody more than she loved me until I learned that she was hard on me because she loved me. She was merely trying to keep me on the right path. Her famous saying in this situation was, "Do it because it is the right thing to do."

Mommie did a lot of things that she didn't want to do because in her heart she thought they were the right thing. She still does. I, on the other hand, ended up leaving your world with transgressions that I now have to be accountable for because I didn't follow her example. I didn't follow the lessons I had been taught in Sunday school either for I knew all too well what the scripture said about not resolving your grudges. For anyone possessing an unforgiving spirit, I advise you to read Ephesians 4:25-27, *"Therefore each of you must put off falsehood and speak truthful to your neighbor, for we are all members of one body. In your anger do not sin. Do not let the sun go down while you are still angry, and do not give the devil a foothold."*

I am thankful that when I died that I didn't leave earth holding any malice against anyone. Had I been harvesting any ill feelings against anyone, I would not have been able to make amends. Just some 'food for thought', "Don't put off for tomorrow what you can do today". Tomorrow is not promised to any man. Actually, the next day is not guaranteed either. Being prideful is not worth your salvation.

Like John, Cher and I had frequently engaged in discussions that stemmed around religious practices and beliefs. That was why I was so anxious to talk to her. I explained to her that I was sorry I had to go but I was with my children and I was happy. I had some books in my arms and she asked me if I was going to school here. I replied,

"Not exactly but you have to learn how to live in this world." It was important to relay messages that deviated in content but not in context. My fear was that if the messages that would eventually find their way to Mommie were the same she might think that there may have been some way that the messengers had spoken with each other. It was important that they did not appear to be mimicking each other's story.

Cher asked me if I had been to see my son. I replied, "No." I became overcome by a feeling of sadness. As I told you before, we miss the loved ones we left behind and I was experiencing some emotional sadness because he wasn't here with me. Although I was happy about the fact that I had been reunited with my other children, the puzzle was incomplete. I hadn't been to see him because I feared that I needed to deal with my emotions first. I was trusting God to give me the strength to face the difficult task of accepting that once it was time to leave him again that I would be able to face that without being left with a heavy heart.

I realize that it may appear that it took me a long time to get around to coming back to see him but time is not measured here the same way that it is there. Nobody worries about time. There really is no need to be concerned about it because it's not like we are going anywhere. We are not on the clock. Nevertheless, after a long deliberation, my son was the next person that I did go to visit.

I felt that I needed to take caution in the deliverance of my messages to my son because it was important to me that my visits not leave him with a broken spirit. The thought of only being able to be near him through his dreams was tough for me. Needless to say, I was thankful to be able to communicate with him on any level that God had allowed me to communicate. I was hoping that my son would awaken after his dream feeling happy to have seen me and realizing that I would always be just a dream away.

When I came to him in his dream, we were sitting on a bench in a park. The sun was shining and there was a gentle breeze blowing through the trees. During my visit with him, I was able to feel his excitement about being able to see me again, even if it was only through a dream. I was certainly overjoyed to be with him again. I began by trying to explain to him too that I didn't want to leave him but it was my time to go. I told him that I loved him. I assured him that I would always be with him, watching over him, and protecting him.

I wasn't certain my son would understand

everything that I was trying to explain to him but knowing Lil Ali like I do, I knew that he would go to my mother, his Nanna, for clarity. I am absolutely not implying that my mother has all of the answers. I simply know my son well enough to say that Nanna is the most constant person in his life. So to her would be where he would go to seek answers to his questions or concerns. Of course he has a girlfriend now. I just thought that I would make him aware that I know that.

I failed to teach Lil Ali to go to God with his problems and concerns. I certainly pray that my mother or someone will teach him. While I am on the subject of things that we as parents often fail to teach our children, parents please explain to your children that you don't have all of the answers to life's mysteries. Teach your children to go to the Creator. Of course, it is important to put into practice what you teach them. Parents should lead by example. I didn't always do that but God entrusts us with those precious souls and gives us specific instructions. *"And ye fathers, provoke not your child to wrath, but bring them up in the nurture and admonition of the Lord"*, *Ephesians 6:4.* Then Proverbs 22:6 reads, *"Train up a child in the way he should go: and when he is old, he will not depart from it."*

I am going to get off of my soapbox for now but don't take it anywhere because I'm not done. Anyway, I was sure that if Lil Ali had any questions about his dream or if he merely wanted to discuss the dream that his Nanna would explain and answer any questions he might have to the best of her ability. I am sure that he remembers me discussing the many revelations that actually unfolded after her telling us about them appearing in her dreams so I mentioned all of my children but I didn't want him to be confused. He was only two years old when I loss the first child and three years old when I had an ectopic pregnancy. He was too young to remember either experience; therefore, I wasn't certain that he would understand what I meant when I told him that we were all together again. Nevertheless, even if he didn't have a clue of what I was talking about, he will know when he gets here who they are because the spiritual being knows and understands far more than the flesh will ever be able to comprehend.

I continued to explain to Lil Ali that where we are is a very beautiful and peaceful place and that we were very happy here. It did concern me that my son might think that I was happier here with his siblings than I was when I was there with him. I truly hoped that he would be able to understand that life's circumstances made me unhappy and that my unhappiness did not have anything to do with him. He was my first born child and my only son. We were bonded by something that was much stronger than Gorilla glue. I love him more than words can say.

I was delighted to share my good news about Lil Ali's sister too. I let him know that in this world Lady Bug is able to walk and talk. After reassuring him that we were okay, it was time to get down to business. I gave him specific instructions which clearly outlined my expectations of him. I let him know that I didn't want him to use my death as an excuse to be nonproductive.

I was in my son's dream for a very long time. He needed to understand that just because I wasn't there with him, I knew what was going on in his life. I didn't want to leave him. Seeing him was bittersweet for me. I assured him that this would not be the last time that he would see me. I told him that I would always be watching over him and that I loved him very much. Then like a cloud of smoke, the dream ended because it was time for me to go. When your dreams seem to be never ending stories, it is because we just can't bear to end our connection with you. Although it is my desire to come to see him every day, I won't do that because I believe that it would not be good for him emotionally. We can't be stumbling blocks here either.

Trust in the Lord with all your heart, and lean not on your own understanding; in all your ways acknowledge Him, and He shall direct your paths.

Proverbs 3:5-6

My youngest brother, Tony, is still coming to me for advice. He has a large portrait of me on his dresser. When you look at that picture, my eyes appear to follow you around the room. My family realized that my eyes would follow them the moment he set the picture up in his room, which by the way, was supposed to be Mommie's picture. I just thought that I would mention that. Whenever he has a dilemma or he is indecisive about something, he will stand in front of my picture and talk to me. I am still giving him advice and direction even from beyond the grave. I was always like a second mother because I was eighteen years old when Mommie gave birth to Tony. My first child didn't come into the world until ten years after Tony was born so Mommie and I shared Tony for ten years.

I was the only sister that he had and when he wanted to talk to someone about "serious stuff" he would always come to me. We both knew that Mommie's upbringing left her old-fashioned and prudish. Her understanding about the ways of my generation was usually stuck on the ground floor but with him the elevator would drop below the basement level. Tony and I developed an incredible bond. Of course, don't think for one second that we didn't have our moments. On the few occasions that we did bump heads, neither one of us would bend. Lord knows that I could hold a grudge for eternity, if you would let me. Of course that was just it, Mommie would never let me. She usually got her way because she had this disapproving look that she would give you. None of her children could take that look.

The next time I visited Tony was out of necessity. He had always been the type of person who needed to be under pressure to function at his best. If he became frustrated, and it didn't take very much for him to become dissatisfied with people or things, he would be quick to give up. He wasn't a fighter like me. He is smart and has so much potential; however, he lacks motivation. The day that he went home so frustrated about school that he broke an expensive piece of equipment he purchased let me know he needed me. We know when the loved ones whom we left behind are suffering with any kind of physical, emotional, or mental anguish. We were spiritually connected in life and we remain spiritually connected to you after we die.

Aside from the fact that Tony is struggling so hard to deal with the harsh reality that he can no longer physically see or feel my presence, I so wish that he would learn to be content with communicating with me spiritually. I became troubled because I knew that he needed comforting. Of course, I was going to do just that but not without chastisement. Since I have been here learning so much from God, I remembered that 1 Corinthians 13:4-7 says, *"Love is patient, love is kind. It does not envy, it does not boast, it is not proud. It does not dishonor others, it is not self-seeking, it is not easily angered, it keeps no record of wrongs. Love does not delight in evil but rejoices with the truth. It always protects, always trusts, always hopes, always perseveres."*

The old me would have given Tony the two-edge sword, tongue lashing of his life. But that evening when he went to sleep, I came to him in a dream. In his dream, I was sitting in a computer lab with my back facing the door. Those of you who know me will laugh because they know how much time I spent on the computer when I was alive. It was my saving grace during those late nights when I was up attending to the needs of Lady Bug. Some of that time should have been spent reading my Bible or praying. Anyway, the building was being evacuated and therefore Tony was going to each floor to make sure that Mommie had gotten out safely. When he finally got to the basement, he saw the computer lab. As he got closer to the door, he could see that there was someone in the room sitting at one of the computers. He thought that it was Mommie. Tony called out to her and when I turned around; he could see that it was me instead. "Oh Kathy! It's you," he said. "I am so happy to see you, Kathy," he replied with this huge grin on his face. I looked at him with this disappointed look and said, "No, you are not. I am so angry with you." I could feel his sadness as he lowered his head and looked down at the floor. I wasn't trying to make him sad but I wanted him to know that with me being gone it was high time that he step up and learn to be more responsible. Since our eldest brother was mentally challenged, he was going to have to fill my shoes, like it or not.

God has a plan for each individual's life. The blueprint was developed long before we touched down. We can easily find ourselves straying off the beaten path because we are disobedient and we want to do things our way. Sometimes God doesn't work fast enough for us but Tony might as well accept the fact that I am not going to let him get off course and neither is God. You can run from God but you can't hide. Of course, freewill can and will create bumps in the road; however, your path would be so much smoother if you heed Joshua's advice, *"Choose you this day whom ye will serve."*

But, beloved, be not ignorant of this one thing, that one day *is* with the Lord as a thousand years, and a thousand years as one day.

2 Peter 3:8

I had been dead for over a year when I finally visited Mommie. She was sick and experiencing a lot of stomach pain. What is important to point out to you is that I knew she was sick. I can't say that she needed me to come to her at that particular time any more than I can say that I needed to be with her at that particular time. Needless to say, it was important to let her know that God would always allow me to be there to comfort her when she needed me.

In her dream, she was in the bathroom sitting on the toilet with her head resting in her hands. I was sitting on the side of the tub. The dream must have felt very real to her because I was wearing the same old dingy white nightshirt that I frequently wore when I was living. It was one of my favorite loungers. Mommie begged me for years to toss it in the trash but I refused to part with it. I loved to wear it because it was comfortable. Anyway, when Mommie saw me from the corner of her eye sitting there on the side of the tub, she didn't act surprised. It was almost like she expected me to be there. Like I would have done had I still been living.

Mommie worried about all of her children, her family, her friends, and their families, and I worried about her. It worries me that she doesn't have another daughter to look after her but Mommie has been blessed to have crossed paths with so many wonderful people. She used to say that God placed people in her life and that she didn't choose them. "Everybody can't be my friend. It's a spiritual thing," she would always say. So, I am going to exhibit some of her faith and trust God to provide her with the things that she needs. I know that her surrogate daughter, Terri, will not forsake her.

Honor your father and your mother, as the LORD your God has commanded you, so that you may live long and that it may go well with you in the land the LORD your God is giving you. Deuteronomy 5:16

I remember when Mommie was pregnant with Tony. She would pray daily to God to let her baby be a boy. She would say, "God, if you are truly a merciful God, please don't give me another girl." I thoroughly understood why she didn't want another girl because I was my mother's problem child, thus earning me the nickname "Miss Too Much." My mother started calling me that name when I was in my early teens. I was very disobedient and disrespectful. I hadn't learned to bridle my tongue.

Mommie should have referred me to *Psalm 141:3 "Set a guard over my mouth, LORD; keep watch over the door of my lips."* When I matured however and began to understand that my mother was doing the best that she knew how to do, I began to appreciate her. When I had children of my own, I understood that I was a good mother because Mommie was a good mother to her children.

I told my mother many times that I knew I had developed the skills I had because she set a good example. Did my mother make mistakes along the way? Of course she did. But one thing that her children appreciated was the fact that she acknowledged her mistakes. She didn't make excuses; instead she took ownership for them. She believed in trying to make things right. As I got older, I began to realize that there were a lot of things about my mother I thought I knew but in all actuality I didn't have a clue. I think that 1 Corinthians 13:11 would best describe my epiphany. It reads, *"When I was a child, I spoke and thought and reasoned as a child. But when I grew up, I put away childish things."* I thank the Lord for placing me in her hands to watch over me.

After I put away those childish things, I began to honor my mother. I started showing her the respect and love that she deserved. I lived my entire life regretting the ugly things I said and had done to my mother. Mommie never held my actions against me. And although she and God had forgiven me, I was never able to forgive myself. Colossians 3:20 says, *"Children, be obedient to your parents in all things, for this is well-pleasing to the Lord."*

I am not only speaking to the minors. I am also talking to all of the people who think that being over the legal age gives them the right to now say and do whatever they want to say and do to their parents. Proverbs 20:20 reads, *"Whoever curses his father or his mother, his lamp shall be put out in obscure darkness."* Respect your parents and you won't have to worry about having to buy a Seeing Eye dog or not seeing that light that I talked about.

My niece, Brianna, has grieved over my death more than any of my other nieces and nephews. I visit her frequently trying to help comfort her. She gets emotional every time anyone talks about me. When I go to visit her through her dreams, I don't stay very long. I just want her to know that I am with her always. Besides, Mommie is always appearing in the dream which interrupts us. Because of that the dream always ends abruptly. I believe this happens for two reasons. The first reason is because my mother has spent her lifetime trying to protect all of her family, in particular, her children and her grandchildren. She knows that Brianna can become overly emotional. It's almost like Mommie is saying okay Kathy that is enough. Then, Mommie could be jealous because I don't visit her frequently through her dreams. She is spoiled like that.

I have a play sister named Terri. I mentioned her earlier in the story. She came into my life when I was in the second grade. She would braid my hair and I was certainly thankful for that because the good Lord knows that Mommie's idea of a hair style was a lop-sided ponytail.

Terri would come every day and walk me to school. As time went on we developed an incredible bond. We became more than best friends, she was like a sister to me. I even referred to her as my big sis. I thank God for bringing Terri into our life. Some people come into your life for a reason, a season, or a lifetime. She became a "life-timer." Her heart is enormous and she is one person whom you can truly depend on. She roars like a lion but she is a pussycat.

I frequently make my presence known at Terri's house too. She knows that it is me. In fact, Terri talks to me frequently like I am standing right there in her presence. When I want her attention, I mess with her alarm system. My purpose, when I visit her in dreams, is to merely be able to give her a visual image of me and let her know that I am always with her. When I was alive, we spent so much time together. We were like two peas in a pod. I always knew that if anything were to happen to me that she would be devastated.

Terri took my death so hard and is still struggling to accept the fact that I am gone. I saw her lying on my cold body and crying. She stayed with me until the coroner got there and carried my corpse away.

The very first time that I went to see Terri was shortly after I had died. I miss her and I can't wait to see her again. Of course, I don't want to rush her time. I do want her to take better care of herself because Lady Bug told me after she died that Terri was sick. She has had a mild stroke since my death. So I want her to work on her health issues. God allows us to have little glimpses into our loved ones' lives. Sometimes we are able to communicate to you things that you need to be made aware of.

For those who live according to the flesh set their minds on the things of the flesh, but those who live according to the Spirit, the things of the Spirit. For the carnally minded is death, but to be spiritually minded is life and peace.

Romans 8:5-6

Life on earth is laborious. Sometimes it seems like some of God's children have it so hard. I always thought that my mother had it hard but I have learned that you can't do enough for God. Before you misunderstand, I am not trying to say that it is impossible to please God. On the contrary, what I mean by that statement is that it is impossible to feel that you could ever repay anyone who made it possible for you to have everlasting life.

Is it even possible to think that you could ever do enough to repay someone who loved you enough to not only give you life once but twice? How many family or friends can you name who would give their life to save yours? Exactly! You couldn't come up with anyone either, could you? People spend their entire lives trying to appease husbands, significant others, children, and parents but we seem to have great difficulty when it comes to doing those things that are pleasing to God. Why is that, I wonder?

So let's just think about the word "carnal." The definition of carnal is that which relates to the body or relates to physical needs. If you don't develop a habit of incorporating prayer, meditation, and Bible study into your daily life, you will find yourself engaging in ungodly pleasures. Let's not forgot that God warns us that He is a jealous God. Don't rob God of time, talent, or tithes.

"For God so loved the world, that he gave his only begotten Son, that whosoever believeth in him should not perish, but have everlasting life." John 3:16

I mentioned earlier how people get caught up in the ways of the world. Nothing on earth is designed to be permanent. Things rust, mold, break, wither, deteriorate, and oh by the way, they die but to believe and have faith in Christ will give you abundant life on earth and eternal life in heaven. John 10:10 says, *"The thief cometh not, but for to steal, and to kill, and to destroy: I am come that they might have life, and that they might have it more*

abundantly." Your abundance will come in the form of love, peace, joy, and happiness.

Notice that I didn't list money. That is because money can create peace and havoc, joy and pain, happiness and sadness, and let's not forget that the love of money is always the root of all evil. It can create ungodly characteristics in people such as greed and dishonesty. 1 Timothy 6:10 tells you, *"For the love of money is the root of all evil: which while some coveted after, they have erred from the faith, and pierced themselves through with many sorrows."*

Money might buy you happiness on earth, but remember what I said, those things that can be bought with money on earth are just temporary and all the money in the world won't do a thing for you up here. If you just happen to be a person who was born into money or you worked hard to acquire your wealth or even better you just happened to be at the right place at the right time, you might be thinking that I mention these things because I was poor. You may even label me a "hater."

I want to believe that I didn't possess a begrudging spirit but if I did, I certainly have no use for that here and neither will your money be useful; therefore, I am suggesting that you read Revelation 3:17-18. It says, *"You say, 'I am rich; I have acquired wealth and do not need a thing.' But you do not realize that you are wretched, pitiful, poor, blind and naked. I counsel you to buy from me gold refined in the fire, so you can become rich; and white clothes to wear, so you can cover your shameful nakedness; and salve to put on your eyes, so you can see."* Those golden streets and pearly gates have already been bought with a price.

Let not your heart be troubled: ye believe in God, believe also in me. In my Father's house are many mansions: if it were not so, I would have told you. I go to prepare a place for you. And if I go and prepare a place for you, I will come again, and receive you unto myself; that where I am, there ye may be also. And whither I go ye know, and the way ye know. Thomas saith unto him, Lord, we know not whither thou goest; and how can we know the way? Jesus saith unto him, I am the way, the truth, and the life: no man cometh unto the Father, but by me. John 14:1-6

Death is inevitable. It is pointless to fear something that you will surely have to face some day. Franklin D. Roosevelt made a profound statement while he was delivering his inaugural address in 1933. He said, "So, first let me assert my firm belief that the only thing we have to fear is...fear itself — nameless, unreasoning, unjustified terror which paralyzes needed efforts to convert retreat into advance." In order to overcome the fear of death, you must read your Bible regularly and talk to God frequently. Prayer is the key.

It is certainly understandable to want to question those things that we don't have answers to. It is normal to fear the unknown; however, what people who fear death need to realize is that unless you ask God to remove the fear, you will remain in bondage. Philippians 4:13 says, *"I can do all things through Christ, which strengtheneth me."* It didn't say some things, it says *all things.* Luke 1:37 reads, *"Nothing is impossible for God",* so if God can do all things then I am wondering why you are still carrying around that burden.

God assures us that His children need not fear death. Why fear losing something that is only temporary anyway? Would it not be better to have something that is permanent? People can often become so engrossed with the simplicity of the carnal lifestyle that they lose sight of what is important. Although, earthly things may offer people much pleasure. It is only temporary. That is why God tells us that we cannot serve two masters. Philippians 1:21-22 says it so well, *"For to me, to live is Christ and to die is gain. If I am to go on living in the body, this will mean fruitful labor for me. Yet what shall I choose? I do not know! I am torn between the two: I desire to depart and be with Christ, which is better by far;"* Eternal life is great! I have no worries. Jesus paid my debts and yours too. Don't take my word for it, read 1 Corinthians 6:20, *"For ye are bought with a price: therefore glorify God in your body, and in your spirit, which are God's."* Then follow that scripture up with Isaiah 44:22, *"I have swept away your offenses like a cloud, your sins like the morning mist. Return to me, for I have redeemed you."*

Now faith is the substance of things hoped for, the evidence of things not seen. Hebrews 11:1

One thing that I am attempting to try to convey to my loved ones and anyone else reading this book is that your loved ones who have left their earthly life are not dead. They simply don't exist in the form that you knew them in but if you just give it a little thought, you might recall having spiritual connections with your loved ones while they were still living. Think about the times that you answered your telephone and the person who called you was on your mind. There may have been times when an individual was on your mind and when you finally took the time out to contact them you discovered that they were ill.

Have you ever loss contact with someone and deeply had a desire to be reunited and then by some strange set of circumstances, you were reconnected? All of those examples could be considered forms of spiritual connections. The spirit doesn't depend on the earthly body to sustain it; it is merely temporarily housed there. So then, why is it hard to believe that an independent agent is capable of operating outside of the human body? The answer to that question might be determined by your personal relationship with God or the lack of. You have to be able to recognize God's efforts to communicate with you through the spirit.

Now, think about the times when something happened in your house that simply just could not be explained. I encountered a few unexplained events before I died. I will share with you one in particular that occurred a few days after my daughter's death. I was awakened early one morning by my son who was frantically babbling about an earthquake occurring during the night. I finally sat up and began to calm him down so that I could understand what the excitement was all about. He kept asking if there had been an earthquake during the night. I hadn't felt anything until he came and disturbed my sleep. When I asked him why he thought that there had been an earthquake he pleaded for me to follow him to his room. When we got to his room and I pushed the door open, I was in shock. It looked like a tornado had struck; even the television was on the floor. When I inspected the rest of the house, everything seemed to be intact. I couldn't explain it then but I understand now because I must confess that

I have created a few occurrences in some of my relatives' homes. My mother can show you evidence of our ability to communicate with you.

I would admonish my mother and anyone that is being hindered because they are afraid of the unknown to continuously pray and to ask God for deliverance. If you love God, then believe in His word. Trust Him. Once you have been set free, you will be able to relate to what the Apostle Paul was saying in 1 Corinthians 15:19, *"If we have hoped in Christ in this life only, we are of all men most to be pitied."*

Jesus' promise to us of salvation can be found in the book of John, chapter 14 in verses 2-3. It reads, *"In my Father's house are many mansions: if it were not so, I would have told you. I go to prepare a place for you. And if I go and prepare a place for you, I will come again, and receive you unto myself; that where I am, there ye may be also."*

God's plan is simple but it is entirely up to each individual to choose the path that they wish to follow. Don't allow your earthly life choices to keep you from reaping heavenly rewards. Heaven is not a state of being. It is a place where everyone should desire to be. In the book of Revelation, chapter 21, the Apostle John describes the reward of dying in Christ. Verses 1 and 4, in particular, declare the beauty and splendor of the ultimate reward that salvation will offer those who accept Christ as their Lord and Savior. It reads, *"And I saw a new heaven and a new earth: for the first heaven and the first earth were passed away; and there was no more sea. And God shall wipe away all tears from their eyes; and there shall be no more death, neither sorrow, nor crying, neither shall there be any more pain: for the former things are passed away."* Reading that scripture should make people yearn to live their lives so that they can inherit the blessings that God has for them. Certainly they would choose Christ if it were not for that red, pitchfork, toting demon but life is about choice. I would like to reiterate that you might want to consider following in the footsteps of Joshua. *"And if it seem evil unto you to serve the LORD, choose you this day whom ye will serve; whether the gods which your fathers served that were on the other side of the flood, or the gods of the Amorites, in whose land ye dwell: but as for me and my house, we will serve the LORD."* Joshua 24:15

For the Spirit God gave us does not make us timid, but gives us power, love and self-discipline. 2 Timothy 1:7

There is a Latin saying, "memento mori", which means remember that you have to die. The body dies daily. The shadow that you see when you walk outside is like a symbolic representation of death. It is like a metaphor. It reminds you that life is followed by death. You can run but you can't hide. Just like death, you can't escape it nor can you control it. It follows you wherever you go. The sun will go down one day never to shine no more. Since death is inevitable, what can you lose by trusting in God's word?

Mommie, more than anything, I want you to know that I will see you again. We will be waiting for you with out-stretched arms when you cross over but until that day, engrave these words in your heart, *"I will lift up mine eyes unto the hills, from whence cometh my help. My help cometh from the LORD, which made heaven and earth."* Psalm 121:1-2

Your Loved Ones Will Be Waiting For You Too!

"For the LORD is good; his mercy is everlasting; and his truth endureth to all generations." Psalm 100:5

AMEN

When I Realized That I Would Never See You Again

ABOUT THE AUTHOR

God built her to withstand the storms of life. Victoria Manuel-Hogan is no stranger to rainy days. She was born in Kentucky, raised in Indiana, and hails from a generation where children were seen and not heard. Victoria used her hidden talents to journal her inner thoughts and feelings. This became the determining factor in Victoria becoming an author. Writing was her way of expressing herself. If you know her, then you know that she always has a lot to say.

Losing her mother at the age of four caused her great-grandmother to be her new example. Victoria developed wisdom and insight which reached far beyond her age. The daily prayer meetings and Bible teachings helped her develop the spiritual relationship that she has with God. She is a passionate matriarch because of the influence that her great-grandmother had in her life.

Victoria has touched the lives of many. She is a loving mother, grandmother, adopted mother, big sister, aunt, cousin, and friend to an infinite amount of grateful recipients. Her dedication to helping and inspiring people around her has been outstanding. She is known for finding a way where there seems to be no way. She is an accomplishment in this thing called life.

Victoria Manuel-Hogan is a published author. Her accomplishments include the book, *When I Realized That I Would Never See You Again*, due to be released in June 2015. In 2009, her poem, *Gone But Not Forgotten*, was published in the book of poems entitled, *Famous Poets of the Heartland*. She has also written numerous children's readers and an autobiography entitled, *Aawww I'm Tellin*, to be released at a later date.

To know her is to love her and in return you receive unconditional love that will forever change your life. Many tribulations delayed her plight to write, but she wants people to understand that even a late start can lead to a triumphant ending.

Submitted by:

Shelley Clanton and Antonio Thomas

CPSIA information can be obtained
at www.ICGtesting.com
Printed in the USA
LVHW082251290321
682919LV00035B/902